Compass^e
Managerial
Practices
Profile

ACTION GUIDE

Compass^e Managerial Practices Profile

ACTION GUIDE

MANUS

Jossey-Bass
Pfeiffer

San Francisco

ISBN: 0-7879-4434-3

Printed in the United States of America.

Published by

350 Sansome Street, 5th Floor
San Francisco, California 94104–1342
(415) 433–1740; Fax (415) 433–0499
(800) 274–4434; Fax (800) 569–0443

Visit our website at: www.pfeiffer.com

Outside of the United States, Jossey-Bass/Pfeiffer products can be purchased from the following Simon & Schuster International Offices:

Simon & Schuster (Asia) Pte Ltd
317 Alexandra Road
#04–01 IKEA Building
Singapore 159965
Asia
65 476 4688; Fax 65 378 0370

Jossey-Bass Pfeiffer
3255 Wyandotte Street East
Windsor, Ontario N8Y 1E9
Canada
888-866-559; Fax 800-605-2665

Prentice Hall
Campus 400
Maylands Avenue
Hemel Hempstead
Hertfordshire HP2 7EZ
United Kingdom
44(0) 1442 881891; Fax 44(0) 1442 882288

Prentice Hall Professional
Locked Bag 507
Frenchs Forest PO NSW 2086
Australia
61 2 9454 2200; Fax 61 2 9453 0089

Prentice Hall/Pfeiffer
P.O. Box 1636
Randburg 2125
South Africa
27 11 781 0780; Fax 27 11 781 0781

Acquiring Editor: Larry Alexander
Director of Development: Kathleen Dolan Davies
Developmental Editor: Marian Prokop
Editor: Rebecca Taff
Senior Production Editor: Dawn Kilgore
Interior Design: Bruce Lundquist
Cover Design: Paula Goldstein

Printing 10 9 8 7 6 5 4 3 2 1

Table of Contents

Compass^e Action Guide

Introduction

This Action Guide is intended to accompany the Compass^e: Managerial Practices Profile questionnaire and participant materials. It provides detailed information about each of the eight leadership and managerial practices measured and is intended to help people who want to improve their use of any practice or to understand it better.

Each chapter defines, gives examples, and presents guidelines on the use of one of the practices. Tips about each practice and lists of recommended readings are also included.

Involving Others

It would be best if men were born with perfect wisdom, but failing this, it can be no dishonor to learn from others when they speak good sense.

—SOPHOCLES

Definition and Examples

Involving Others means checking with people before making changes that affect them, encouraging participation in decision making, and allowing others to influence decisions.

Examples of Involving Others include:

- Encouraging people to suggest improvements and innovations, such as better ways to do work or new or improved products;
- Consulting with people to hear their reactions and suggestions before making major changes that will affect them;
- Encouraging people to help determine the best way to carry out an assignment or accomplish an objective;
- Listening carefully to any concerns people express about proposals or plans without becoming defensive; and
- Modifying proposals or plans to deal with people's concerns and to incorporate their suggestions.

Notes

By Involving Others one can improve the quality of decisions and gain commitment to them. One can also develop the decision-making skills of other people in the organization. Use of this practice must be based on a genuine desire for people's input, and their input must be valued and used, or one's ability to influence people will diminish over time.

A study conducted in 1994 (Freeman & Rogers, 1994) indicated that the vast majority of people in organizations want more involvement and an increased say in company decisions that affect them. Employees believe that increased influence will give them greater job satisfaction and improve competitive performance

Inviting participation in decision making is not an all-or-nothing affair; the degree of participation falls along a continuum. Some of the ways in which others can be encouraged to participate in decision making include:

- Revising a tentative decision after listening to people's concerns;
- Asking for advice from others before making a decision; and
- Asking a group to make a decision in conjunction with the manager or project leader.

Participation may be encouraged at any stage of the decision-making process: diagnosing the problem; identifying alternative solutions; evaluating those alternatives; planning for implementation; or implementing the chosen solution.

The success of a decision depends on both the quality of the decision and the acceptance of the decision by those who will be affected by it.

Decision Quality

The highest-quality decision is the best alternative among those available—the one that would solve a problem and have the best results if implemented properly. For example, a decision is high-quality if the most efficient work process is selected from among several alternatives or if a critical assignment is given to the most qualified person.

Decision quality is jeopardized by any of the following:

- Analyzing the problem in an unsystematic way;
- Jumping to conclusions about the cause of a problem;
- Focusing on who is to blame for the problem rather than on solving it ("scapegoating");
- Inhibiting creative ideas;
- Failing to recognize unfavorable information;
- Being overly optimistic in appraising a particular option ("wishful thinking");
- Deciding too quickly; or
- Avoiding difficult choices.

Participation by direct reports or colleagues will not increase the quality of a decision unless they have relevant information, ideas, or analytical skills. If all the information needed to solve a problem is already known, Involving Others will not improve the quality of the decision, although it may improve the likelihood that the decision will be accepted.

More input is probably necessary if the problem is complex. Complex situations have one or more of the following characteristics:

- The cause of the problem is not obvious;
- There is no clear best solution;
- Any solution is likely to have some undesirable side effects; or
- Any choice requires some trade-offs among potential benefits.

Acceptance of the Decision

Acceptance, the other requirement for a successful decision, is the extent to which people who must implement the decision believe in it and are motivated to make it work, regardless of the obstacles. If a manager must depend on other people to implement a decision, those people's apathy, resistance, or inability to accept it may lead to its failure, regardless of how high the decision quality is.

Involving Others increases acceptance of decisions. When people have substantial involvement in a decision, they tend to assume ownership of it and try to make it successful. Some reasons for this follow:

- Participation allows people to understand the nature of a problem and the reasons why a particular alternative is accepted or rejected;
- Participation provides an opportunity to voice concerns and bring about a solution that addresses these concerns; and
- When people make a group decision through a process they consider to be legitimate, others in the group may encourage or pressure any reluctant members to do their part in implementing it.

When It Is Most Useful

Involving Others is most useful in the following situations:

- When people have relevant knowledge and information needed to solve problems and make good decisions;
- If the people participating in decision making share your objectives and are willing to cooperate in making a good decision;
- When the one in charge is highly dependent on the others to approve or implement a decision or change;
- If there is enough time to hold the necessary meetings or conversations; or
- When a coach or manager is willing to allow selected individuals or a group to participate to improve their decision-making skills, despite the risk that decision quality will be lower. (In this case, the benefits of learning from one's mistakes should be greater than the risks associated with making lower-quality decisions.)

Tips

Here are some tips for Involving Others:

- Identify people with relevant expertise to help solve a problem; consult with them individually or invite them to attend a group meeting.
- Hold special meetings to obtain reactions from people who will be affected by a decision in order to identify any concerns that may have been overlooked.
- Encourage people to suggest better ways to do the work or ways to improve products and services.
- Stimulate and reward creativity; protect and nurture creative ideas and solutions.
- Try to use suggested improvements whenever possible; if a suggestion is not used, thank the contributor and explain why it was not feasible.
- Encourage critical evaluation of proposals before finalizing them.
- Appoint a "devil's advocate" to look for weaknesses in an important plan or proposal, then present a systematic critique to the group.
- Hold a "second chance" meeting to give people time to reconsider a major decision before finalizing it.
- Downplay evaluative responses; listen carefully to suggestions or criticisms without becoming defensive or angry.
- Ask questions about people's concerns or suggestions to ensure that you understand them.
- Summarize progress in a group discussion; work for consensus on a solution.
- Use the "itemized response" technique when reacting to input. When someone offers an idea or suggestion, first tell the person what you liked about it. Then, if you have any concerns, explain and discuss them. This simple but powerful technique lets people know that you value their opinions, serves to maintain their self-esteem, and preserves the useful aspects of an idea so that they can be built upon.

Readings

Belasco, J.A., & Stayer, R.C. (1993). *Flight of the buffalo: Soaring to excellence, learning to let employees lead.* New York: Warner Books.

Bennis, W., & Biederman, P.W. (1997). *Organizing genius: The secrets of creative collaboration.* Reading, MA: Addison-Wesley.

Freeman, R.B, & Rogers, J. (1994). *Worker Representation and Participation Survey; Report on the Findings,* Princeton Research Associates.

Parker, G.M. (1994). *Cross-functional teams.* San Francisco: Jossey-Bass.

Schatz, K., & Schatz, L. (1986). *Managing by influence.* Englewood Cliffs, NJ: Prentice-Hall.

Vroom, V.H., & Jago, A.G. (1988). *The new leadership: Managing participation in organizations.* Englewood Cliffs, NJ: Prentice- Hall.

Yukl, G. (1998). *Leadership in organizations.* Englewood Cliffs, NJ: Prentice-Hall.

Zenger, J.H., Musselwhite, E., Hurson, K., & Perrin, C. (1994). *Leading teams: Mastering the new role.* Burr Ridge, IL: Irwin Professional.

Building Relationships

Corporate entrepreneurs often have to pull in what they need for their innovation from other departments or areas, from peers over whom they have no authority and who have the choice about whether or not to ante up their knowledge, support, or resources, to invest in and help the innovator. . . . For many, relationships with people in other areas are essential to their success.

—ROSABETH MOSS KANTER

Definition and Examples

Building Relationships is defined as developing contacts with people who are a source of information and support and maintaining those contacts through periodic visits, telephone calls, correspondence, and attendance at meetings and other events.

Examples of Building Relationships include:

- Maintaining contact with people in the organization who can be useful sources of information, resources, and political support;
- Keeping in touch with people outside the organization who can provide information about important developments and events;
- Maintaining good working relationships with people whose cooperation and support are important for providing information, assistance, political support, or resources;
- Forming alliances with people in different parts of the organization to work toward mutual objectives; and
- Meeting with important clients or customers to discover how to better satisfy their needs.

Notes

Relationship-building behavior is used to develop cooperative bonds with others both inside and outside the immediate work unit, including colleagues, the supervisor's boss, people who report to direct reports, customers, suppliers, trade contacts, and even competitors.

Building Relationships is an effective way to gather relevant information and support strategic initiatives. It can also help to build one's power and influence with people who are under no formal obligation to cooperate.

Working to develop and maintain relationships can support other leadership and managerial practices, especially Recognizing and Involving Others, and can be helpful in Managing Conflict. Coaching can also be seen as a very specific form of Building Relationships.

When It Is Most Useful

Building Relationships is most useful in the following situations:

- When working in large organizations or in companies stressing cross-functional cooperation;
- If the job requires people to work with others outside the organization, such as marketing, sales, and purchasing positions;
- In changing situations, such as when new products are developed, new markets are targeted, or new regulatory laws are passed; or
- When people are dependent on others for information or resources.

When to Use

Increase or improve your use of Building Relationships if you:

- Rarely receive inquiries from co-workers or from people outside your work unit;
- Have little involvement in professional activities related to your job;
- Find it difficult to determine where to find help in your organization;
- Learn about changes in your organization only through official communication channels; or
- Spend little time dealing with co-workers or with others outside your immediate work unit.

You may have little need to build relationships if you:

- Spend a good portion of time at work talking about non-work activities;
- Find very little time to devote to actual work because you are too busy networking; or
- Are using your job more to improve your social life than your career.

Tips

Here are some tips for Building Relationships:

- Use a variety of sources, both inside and outside the organization, to obtain information:
  - *Internal sources:* Information on the progress of work-unit operations from reports, observations, and informal conversations with colleagues, direct reports, and other employees.
  - *External sources:* Information on market changes, competitive behavior, technological developments, and general market conditions from customers, suppliers, trade contacts (consultants, bankers, or people in other companies), and from attending conferences and trade shows, reading periodicals, and joining trade associations.
- Join a professional association related to your work and attend scheduled meetings, lunches, and other events.
- Share information with others who may find it useful.
- Show gratitude and appreciation for any favors extended (consistent with company policy) and reciprocate at the appropriate time.
- Provide appropriate recognition, praise, or congratulations to others both inside and outside your work group. Send congratulatory letters, notes, etc.

- Attend trade shows or professional conferences and meetings; work to make contacts and friendships.
- Participate in recreational and leisure activities with business associates.
- Take an interest in the personal details of people's lives, both inside and outside the organization. Jot down details and refer to them later.

Readings

Baker, W.E. (1994). *Networking smart*. New York: McGraw-Hill.

Kaplan, R.E. (1984, Spring). Trade routes: The manager's network of relationships. *Organizational Dynamics, 12.*

Lipnack, J., & Stamps, J. (1993). *The team net factor*. Essex Junction, VT: Oliver Wight Publications.

Luthans, F., Hodgetts, R.M., & Rosenkrantz, S.A. (1988). *Real managers*. Cambridge, MA: Ballinger.

Peters, T. (1992). *Liberation management*. New York: Alfred A. Knopf.

Coaching

Virtually all of the successful and effective executives I have known have had two or more mentoring relationships early in their careers. Some have had upwards of a dozen people whom they were able to rely on for different needs—some provided important contacts, others gave key information in specific areas, and still others taught them certain valued skills.

—JOHN KOTTER

Definition and Examples

Coaching is defined as facilitating someone's skill and career development by providing support and being helpful and patient.

Examples of Coaching include:

- Giving people encouragement and support when they have a difficult and stressful task or responsibility;
- Providing extra instruction to help people improve their job skills or learn new ones;
- Being patient and helpful when giving complicated explanations or instructions;
- Providing people with opportunities to develop their skills and demonstrate what they can do (for example, by involving them in special assignments); and
- Helping people learn from their mistakes.

Notes

Coaching is related to Building Relationships and can be used with colleagues and other co-workers as well as with direct reports. Coaching can improve direct reports' performance and chances for promotion. Coaching relationships are mutually beneficial, yet many people do not realize that Coaching also can promote their own careers. By developing their direct reports, managers can gain more time to focus on other duties; similarly, coaches of colleagues or co-workers can improve their own capabilities and enhance their power bases in their organizations.

Coaching becomes self-reinforcing. Employees who have the opportunity to work under the "wings" of experienced co-workers gain valuable advice early in their careers and are likely to incorporate Coaching into their own work styles. As their careers progress, they are likely to serve as mentors for less-experienced employees.

When Coaching behavior is prevalent in an organization's culture, stronger work teams, better work-unit performance, and a less stressful climate usually result. Power struggles, infighting, and other problems may also be reduced. Competition is channeled where it belongs—outside the organization—rather than toward other people within the company.

Roles of a Coach

It is important to understand and differentiate between the two main roles of a coach: *evaluator* and *mentor*. As an evaluator, a coach assesses and passes judgment on performance. As a mentor, a coach helps the person reach his or her highest potential. In some situations, coaches may need to suspend judgment, listen carefully to the needs expressed, and be ready to offer training and advice. As a coach, it is important to:

- Create a climate that permits a free-flowing dialogue;
- Form positive relationships based on mutual respect and trust; and
- Guide people to discover their own insights through questioning.

Good coaches need the following skills to be effective:

- *Observation:* Monitor the person's performance closely. Rely on direct observations of his or her performance as well as written reports, budget performance, and the opinions of others.
- *Analysis:* Identify opportunities for people to enhance their capabilities and improve performance. In the case of direct reports, decide whether they need a formal training program, an informal Coaching session, or some other developmental opportunity. Be sure they know what is expected of them and have at least a general idea about how to reach their objectives.
- *Listening:* Listen to the person's needs and concerns. When exploring ways to improve performance, ask questions to stimulate thinking and encourage suggestions. For example, rather than summarily discounting an idea that you disagree with, probe further by asking, "What other options are there?" "What have others done in a similar situation?"
- *Giving Feedback:* Here are some guidelines for using this skill:
  - *Be specific, not general.* If someone's performance is not up to standard, provide specific examples, saying something like, "Jim was disappointed that you didn't get back to him quickly enough. What can you do to assure him of your total cooperation in the future?"
  - *Be descriptive, not evaluative.* For example, if a team member made a poor presentation to management, focus specifically on what he or she might have done differently: "Try to talk more slowly next time and maintain eye contact with your audience." The person needs specific suggestions for improvement, not disapproval.
  - *Do not give feedback when you are upset.* Doing so will serve no constructive purpose. Wait until you have cooled down.
- *Counseling:* A coach can also help employees deal with career problems, such as lack of advancement, personal conflicts, burnout, or skill deficiencies and personal problems affecting work performance. Help the person to identify and express his or her concerns and feelings, help to analyze the reasons for the problem, and provide information that will help him or her solve it. If necessary, refer the person to professionals who can provide assistance and help to identify alternatives.

When It Is Most Useful

Coaching is most useful in the following situations:

- When people share the basic goals of their work unit and organization and have the desire to succeed, but are relatively inexperienced;
- When the work is difficult and members of the work unit are frustrated and discouraged by temporary setbacks or lack of progress;
- When the organization is large, has a complex structure, and operates in a fast-changing environment;
- If the prospective coach has a wealth of useful information about the organization, a good performance record, and control of critical organizational resources; or
- If direct reports need guidance and counseling to chart a sound career path.

When to Use

You probably need to increase or improve your use of Coaching if:

- The skills of fellow team members or direct reports do not improve over time;
- Direct reports or colleagues are unaware of possible career tracks in the organization;
- People you work with do not receive key assignments and promotions that become available in the organization;
- Co-workers or direct reports are not satisfied with their career progress;
- Upper-level management is unaware of the performance of your direct reports;
- Absenteeism and turnover are high (although other factors may also be at work);
- People never question you or offer suggestions on how work unit policies, programs, and activities can be improved (suggesting that their relationships with you are very formal);
- You rarely perform informal evaluations of direct reports' performance; or
- You lack confidence in colleagues' or direct reports' abilities to complete assigned tasks.

Too much Coaching can also have adverse effects on people. You may need to use less Coaching if co-workers or direct reports perceive you as overprotective; this may be a sign that you tend to smother them, not giving them a chance to make a mistake.

Tips

Here are some tips for Coaching:

- Ensure privacy and freedom from interruptions; do not conduct a Coaching session in a public place or where you may be interrupted.
- Pick an opportune time; do not begin immediately after someone's anxiety-filled presentation. He or she may not be ready to accept advice at that time. However, do not delay the Coaching session for more than a day after the event. Set up a time to talk so that it will not slip your mind.
- Coaching does not always need to be done in a formal session; informal coaching during the course of a work day can also be effective.
- Use coaches or mentors you have had in the past as examples. Determine what each did that was particularly helpful. Use the good coaches as models for Coaching others.

- Notice others in your organization who are particularly good coaches; ask them how they do it.
- If you are a manager, take time to learn about the career paths of your direct reports and about where they would like to be in the future. Stress the individual's responsibility for managing his or her own career and determine how you might support these efforts.
- Look for training opportunities that will help employees develop their skills.
- Organize events during which people in your team or work unit have the opportunity to meet higher-level management.
- Be a mentor to people who are valuable to the organization, not just to the people who are similar to you.
- Spend some time with each direct report and important colleague to learn about him or her personally; find out about his or her interests, recreational activities, family, and hobbies.
- Watch someone you consider to be a good listener. Determine what he or she does and try to do the same.
- Whenever feasible, make a special effort to help an employee who seeks assistance with a job-related problem or unusual work demands.
- Help to build the self-esteem of people you work with by providing recognition and boosting their confidence when they are faced with a challenging task or problem.
- Be patient and helpful when giving instructions or directions.
- Provide constructive criticism and help people learn from their mistakes.
- Be sensitive to people's moods and feelings. Learn to recognize when someone is upset, frustrated, angry, or depressed.
- Use good timing and pick up on cues about when to approach and when to back off.

Readings

Brief, A.P., Schuler, R.S., & Van Sell, M. (1981). *Managing job stress.* Boston: Little-Brown.

Cavaleri, S., & Fearon, D. (1996). *Managing organizations that learn.* Cambridge, MA: Blackwell Publishers.

Daniels, A.C. (1993). *Bringing out the best in people.* New York: McGraw-Hill.

Lunding, F.J., Clements, G.L., & Perkins, D.S. (1978, July-August). Everyone who makes it has a mentor. *Harvard Business Review, 56,* 135–147.

Miller, J.B., & Brown, P.B. (1994). *The corporate coach: How to build a team of loyal customers and happy employees.* New York: Harper Business.

Mink, O.G., Keith, O.Q., & Mink, B.P. (1993). *Developing high-performance people.* Reading, MA: Addison-Wesley.

Noe, R.A. (1991). Mentoring relationships for employee development. In J.W. Jones, B.D. Steffy, & D.W. Bray (Eds.), *Applying psychology in business: The managers's handbook.* Lexington, MA: Lexington Press.

Orth, C.D., Wilkinson, H.E., & Benfari, C. (1987, Spring). The manager's role as coach and mentor. *Organizational Dynamics, 15,* 66–74.

Yukl, G. (1990). *Skills for managers and leaders.* Englewood Cliffs, NJ: Prentice Hall.

Yukl, G. (1998). *Leadership in organizations.* Englewood Cliffs, NJ: Prentice-Hall.

Recognizing

Money alone says you did a good job—it doesn't say why. Recognition provides an opportunity to say why, to express appreciation, and to ensure that people will keep doing their best.

—ALLYN KEISER, FORMER EXECUTIVE VICE PRESIDENT
OF CANADIAN IMPERIAL BANK OF COMMERCE

Definition and Examples

Recognizing involves giving praise and showing appreciation to others for effective performance, significant achievements, and special contributions.

Examples of Recognizing include:

- Complimenting people for demonstrating unusual creativity, initiative, persistence, or skill in performing a task;
- Giving people credit for helpful ideas and suggestions;
- Expressing personal appreciation when a person does something that requires a special effort;
- Explaining why a person's performance was good by citing specific examples of effective behavior, recognizing important contributions, and acknowledging difficult obstacles that were overcome; and
- Praising improvements in performance.

Notes

The primary purpose of Recognizing is to reinforce desirable behavior, but secondary objectives include improving relationships, increasing job satisfaction, and building commitment to the organization. Although it is most common to think of recognition as being given by a manager to direct reports, one can also recognize a colleague or a supervisor. Recognizing can be an important and effective part of Building Relationships. *Praise, awards,* and *ceremonies* are the most frequently used methods for Recognizing.

Using Praise

Instead of making a general comment, explain specifically what you liked. Indicate the basis for your judgment, point out examples of special effort or effective behavior, and explain why the person's accomplishments are important to you and to the organization. When praising someone for good suggestions, explain how the person's ideas were used and how they benefited the organization or project.

Specific praise shows the person that you actually know what he or she has done. In addition, giving specific examples highlights the behaviors that you value and encourages the person to repeat those behaviors in the future.

Using Awards

Many awards are symbols of recognition—for example, a framed certificate, a letter of commendation, a trophy, pin, ribbon, or badge, an article in the company newsletter, or a picture of the person on an "Employee of the Month" plaque displayed in a prominent place.

Awards are also more effective when the specific accomplishments or contributions are cited so that other people will know why the award was given and understand that it was based on meaningful criteria rather than favoritism or arbitrary judgments. Awards that are highly visible add to the benefits of private praise, because others can share in the process of commending the person and showing their appreciation.

Using Ceremonies

A ceremony or special event ensures that a person's accomplishments are made public and also celebrated by other members of the organization. When top management attends, special ceremonies honoring particular employees and teams have more symbolic value than announcements in a newsletter or on a bulletin board. Ceremonies demonstrate appreciation for outstanding performance.

Guidelines for Recognizing

The following are some guidelines for Recognizing others:

- Decide what kind of accomplishments should be recognized. People often limit the practice to major achievements. Recognition can be provided for a variety of other things as well, including:

  - Demonstration of initiative and extra effort;
  - Achievement of challenging performance goals;
  - Personal sacrifices made to accomplish a task or objective;
  - Helpful suggestions and innovative ideas for improving efficiency;
  - Improvement in productivity or the quality of the work unit's products or services;
  - Special efforts to help someone else deal with a problem; or
  - Significant contributions to the success of other people or teams.

- Identify the types of behavior, contributions, and accomplishments that are important for the success of the organization and are consistent with your values and ideals. Spend some time each day looking for examples of effective behavior to recognize. Periodic awards such as "Employee of the Week" provide a way to identify effective performance regularly.

- Recognize individual improvement to encourage future improvement. Do it in a way that communicates expectations of continuing progress toward excellence. (This is particularly relevant for new employees and for employees who may lack self-confidence.)

- Recognize efforts that are *not* successful. One company fires a cannon to celebrate "perfect failure" when research scientists terminate a failing project instead of prolonging it at greater cost to the company. In a similar way, thank a person who suggests an improvement that turns out not to be feasible, and explain why the idea could not be implemented. This will encourage that person to continue making suggestions in the future.
- Be generous. Contributions and achievements by all employees at all levels should be recognized, regardless of their visibility and the ease of measuring their progress. Indicators of successful performance can be set for every job.
- Recognize many winners, rather than a few. It is better to provide awards for the top 25 percent of sales representatives rather than the top 10 percent, and better to give an award to everyone who exceeds a challenging performance standard rather than just to the person with the best performance. Extreme forms of competition and resentment can develop in people who perform exceptionally well but receive little or no recognition. To achieve the desired benefits from Recognizing, however, give more recognition to those with the very best performance.

When and How Often

Recognition for performance should not be limited to quarterly or annual ceremonies. Measure performance at shorter time intervals, such as monthly or weekly. Identify effective behavior and provide recognition for it promptly. One of the benefits of "management by walking around" is that you can see examples of good work and provide immediate praise.

On the other hand, Recognizing should not be easily predictable or overused. It becomes "stale" and may appear manipulative if a person is praised every day for the same behavior. It is not necessary to provide recognition every time a person does a routine task well or exceeds a short-term performance standard.

When It Is Most Useful

Recognizing is most useful in the following situations:

- When performance is determined by an individual's skill and motivation, rather than by luck or uncontrolled factors;
- When people lack self-confidence and experience in doing their jobs; or
- If people receive little performance feedback from co-workers, clients, or customers.

Tips

Here are some tips for Recognizing:

- Be sincere.
- Pay particular attention to attempts to improve; recognize even small improvements.
- Establish ways for employees to recognize one another: suggestion boxes, employee-sponsored awards, and so on.
- Ensure that there are ways for people to hear praise and accolades that come from outside sources such as clients or vendors.
- Ask for the good news as well as the bad. Ask people to identify what has been

going well; then take time to celebrate accomplishments.

- Remember that recognition of groups and teams can be particularly effective.
- Encourage people to recognize their own accomplishments; this can help them develop their own internal recognition and reward systems and increase their job satisfaction and self-esteem.
- Avoid pairing a request with a compliment; this smacks of manipulation and will not build a foundation of trust and respect.
- Inappropriate use of recognizing will reduce its perceived value and your ability to influence others.

Readings

Fromm, B., & Schlesinger, L. (1993). *The real heroes of business (and not a CEO among them)*. New York: Currency Doubleday.

Kouzes, J.M., & Posner, B.Z. (1987). *The leadership challenge: How to get extraordinary things done in organizations*. San Francisco: Jossey-Bass.

Kouzes, J.M., & Posner, B.Z. (1995). *The leadership challenge: How to keep getting extraordinary things done in organizations*. San Francisco: Jossey-Bass.

Levering, R., Moskowitz, M., & Katz, M. (1984). *The 100 best companies to work for in America*. Reading, MA: Addison-Wesley.

Nelson, B. (1994). *1001 ways to reward employees*. New York: Workman Publishing.

Managing Conflict

Out of discord comes the fairest harmony.

—HERACLITUS

Definition and Examples

Managing Conflict is defined as facilitating the constructive resolution of differences and encouraging cooperation, teamwork, and identification with the organizational unit.

Examples of Managing Conflict include:

- Encouraging frank and open discussion of a disagreement;
- Attempting to resolve disagreements in a constructive manner by mutual problem solving;
- Trying to understand the other person's point of view when there is a disagreement by listening carefully, asking questions, not refuting others' points, and summarizing others' positions to check for understanding; and
- Proposing a reasonable compromise to resolve a disagreement.

Notes

The primary purpose of Managing Conflict is to build and maintain cooperative working relationships. When conflict is managed effectively, everyone in the work unit has an integral role to play and is committed to a common goal.

Managing Conflict is related to both Building Relationships and Coaching, because these practices promote productive relationships among people in an organization. Recognizing and rewarding teamwork among group members also sends a powerful signal about the importance of working as a team and resolving differences.

An overall organizational climate of trust, positive feelings, and a sense of responsibility is essential for conflict to be managed productively. People also must be able to accept differing viewpoints.

When It Is Most Useful

Managing Conflict is most useful in the following situations:

- When people working in close proximity are under stress for long periods of time;
- When there is competition for rewards, status, and/or organizational resources;
- When other work units have different goals and priorities; or
- If differences in values, time perspectives, objectives, or background and training cause suspicion, misunderstanding, and hostility.

When To Use

You may need to increase or improve your use of Managing Conflict if you can answer "yes" to one or more of the following questions:

- Does your work unit seem to be divided into factions?
- Is there overt hostility among staff members?
- Are people afraid or reluctant to express opposing points of view?
- Do the same issues tend to come up repeatedly?

The presence of any of these symptoms does not automatically mean that Managing Conflict is the only remedy to pursue, but it does suggest that it should be considered.

If it seems as though people are relying on you to mediate all of their disagreements, rather than working things out themselves, you may need to rely on the technique less.

Tips

Here are some behaviors that can be incorporated into your work style to help create and facilitate conflict management:

- Always encourage critical thinking and constructive disagreement.
- Recognize and reward individuals when they are cooperative and collaborative.
- Encourage group interactions by having a group meal periodically, either in the workplace or offsite. Working lunches are an effective way to bring members together informally to discuss problems and opportunities facing the work unit. Involve everyone as much as possible in the conversation.
- Reinforce the importance of having people listen to one another. Hold periodic group meetings that focus on enhancing communication among employees.
- Encourage different team members to assume leadership roles from time to time. The head of the group should not dominate discussions.
- When a decision has been reached and action is ready to be taken, ask people to agree on specific tasks, objectives, and deadlines.

Readings

Katzenbach, J.R., & Smith, D.K. (1993). *The wisdom of teams.* Boston: Harvard University Press.

Lipnack, J., & Stamps, J. (1993). *The team net factor.* Essex Junction, VT: Oliver Wight Publications.

Tjosvold, D. (1993). *Learning to manage conflict: Getting people to work together productively.* New York: The Free Press.

Wall, S.J., & Wall, S.R. *The new strategists: Creating leaders at all levels.* New York: The Free Press.

Wellins, R.S., Byham, W.C., & Wilson, J.M. (1991). *Empowered teams.* San Francisco: Jossey-Bass.

Yukl, G. (1998). *Leadership in organizations.* Englewood Cliffs, NJ: Prentice-Hall.

Zenger, J.H., Musselwhite, E., Hurson, K., & Perrin, C. (1994). *Leading teams: Mastering the new role.* Burr Ridge, IL: Irwin Professional Publishing.

# Influencing

Used well, influence builds strong relationships between people in every business and across every function.

—STEPHEN J. WALL AND SHANNON RYE WALL

Definition and Examples

Influencing involves using techniques that appeal to reason, values, or emotion to generate enthusiasm for the work, commitment to task objectives, or compliance with requests. Examples of Influencing include:

- Talking in a persuasive manner about the importance of achieving excellence in strategically important areas;
- Developing enthusiasm for a task or project by appealing to people's pride in accomplishing a challenging task, beating competitors, or doing something never done before;
- Describing a clear and appealing vision of what can be accomplished with people's cooperation and support;
- Making persuasive arguments to gain support for a proposed project, policy, or plan; and
- Inspiring people to greater effort by setting an example of dedication and hard work.

Notes

In addition to its value for motivating direct reports, Influencing is useful for interactions with colleagues, bosses, and outsiders. Influencing can take many forms, but two major categories are *reasoning* and *inspiring*. Consulting is also a very powerful Influencing tool.

Reasoning

Reasoning involves using logical arguments and factual evidence to persuade people that your strategy, proposal, or request is viable and likely to help the business achieve its goals. Reasoning is used extensively in business. In fact, people use this approach in over two-thirds of their attempts to influence others (Yukl, Falbe & Youn, 1993).

Reasoning may include such behaviors as explaining the reasons for a request, describing how the other person would benefit if he or she supported you, or providing evidence to show that your plan or proposal is likely to succeed. For example, if you are proposing that your business embark on a new strategy, you could refer to a report containing positive results from a pilot study or to a market survey showing that customers would respond well to a new product or innovation. You could also provide documentation about expected costs and benefits or explain how the approach was used successfully in the past.

Another aspect of effective reasoning is anticipating people's concerns and dealing with them directly. Review some possible shortcomings of your proposal and show how they might be overcome. Explain how you plan to avoid problems, overcome obstacles, and minimize risks.

Reasoning is used more frequently when people are trying to convince those who are in a higher position on the organizational chart than when they are dealing with their colleagues on the same level or with people who report to them. This may be because people are accustomed to the idea that they must convince a boss, but believe that simply telling their direct reports what to do is sufficient.

Even though reasoning is, in general, one of the most effective ways to influence people, it cannot be the only way. Although logic may be compelling for many people, others are influenced more by appeals to their emotions and values. In addition, true commitment, as opposed to mere compliance, engages the heart as well as the mind. Because of this, reasoning is often combined with other approaches by the most influential leaders.

Inspiring

Reasoning appeals to the head, but inspiring appeals to the heart. Inspiring develops enthusiasm and commitment by linking proposals to people's values, hopes, and ideals. Values that can be particularly inspiring include the desire to accomplish something worthwhile, to do something exceptional, or to participate in an exciting effort to make things better.

We tend to think of inspirational people as larger than life: world leaders, popes, or renowned humanitarians. However, think of the people who have inspired you. The list probably includes people who are not famous, but who changed your life in an important way. Inspiring is not just the work of those who give speeches or those at the top of an organization. It is a powerful Influencing tool that can be used by people at all levels.

Inspiring is very effective when building commitment, but difficult for many to learn to use. Inspiring need not be done with great fanfare. A quiet one-on-one conversation can be just as effective. If you know that a colleague values the recognition of other experts in his or her field, ask him or her to join a new product development team, emphasizing that there will be opportunities to publish the team's work in a professional journal. If you know that your boss cares a great deal about environmental issues, ask for his or her support for a new product idea, stressing that the new product will be environmentally friendly.

These examples illustrate one key to inspiring effectively: understanding people's values in order to appeal to them. A common mistake is to assume that everyone's values are similar. Appealing to a person's desire for achievement if he or she is really more concerned with balancing work and family time is not likely to be effective.

One obvious way to find out what people really do value is to ask them: "What's most important to you about your job?" "What do you like best about it?" "What do you like least?" Another way is to pay attention to their behavior—what makes them excited? How do they spend their discretionary time at work? The more you know about the values of the people you work with, the easier it will be to link their needs and hopes to the work to be done.

Influencing is built on strong relationships with specific people. Its foundation is trust, which takes time to build and a series of interactions to develop and grow. When used well, influence is not a sneaky, manipulative ploy to trick other people into doing what you want. The best influencers are overt about their desire to gain your support. They admit that they are trying to convince you and truly believe that you will both be well served by the approach they advocate.

When It Is Most Useful

Influencing is most useful in the following situations:
- When an organization is in a state of turmoil and when people are confused about what direction to take;
- When people work across functions or rely on others over whom they have no authority to get work done;
- When the work is difficult and members of the work unit are likely to become frustrated and discouraged by the lack of progress; or
- When the organization is pursuing a high-risk strategy, such as market penetration or introducing an entirely new product.

Tips

Here are some tips for Influencing:
- State your proposals clearly, highlighting the evidence for why you believe the action will be successful.
- Present supporting ideas as benefits, not just as facts.
- Use colorful, emotional language, with metaphors, symbols, and slogans.
- Build confidence in the capacity of the work unit or team to overcome obstacles and accomplish a challenging and important objective.
- Use ceremonies to celebrate successes and build team identity.
- Use symbolic actions to emphasize key values and demonstrate commitment to a strategy or vision.
- Model desirable behaviors and lead by example.
- Listen without interrupting and frequently check for understanding when you speak.
- Ask for and build on suggestions while your proposal is still tentative.

Readings

Bellman, G. (1992). *Getting things done when you are not in charge.* San Francisco: Berrett-Koehler.

Conger, J.A. (1989). *The charismatic leader: Behind the mystique of exceptional leadership.* San Francisco: Jossey-Bass.

Kotter, J. (1985). *Power and influence.* New York: The Free Press.

Kouzes, J.M., & Posner, B.Z. (1993). *Credibility.* San Francisco: Jossey-Bass.

Schatz, K., & Schatz, L. (1986). *Managing by influence.* Englewood Cliffs, NJ: Prentice-Hall.

Tichy, N.M., & Devanna, M.A. (1986). *The transformational leader.* New York: John Wiley.

Wall, S.J., & Wall, S.R. (1995). *The new strategists: Creating leaders at all levels.* New York: The Free Press.

Yukl, G. (1998). *Leadership in organizations.* Englewood Cliffs, NJ: Prentice-Hall.

Yukl, G., Falbe, C.M., & Youn, J.Y. (1993). Patterns of influence behavior for managers. *Group and Organization Management, 18,* 5–28.

Clarifying

The most devoted adherents of an organization will quit it, if its system results in inadequate, contradictory, inept orders, so that they cannot know who is who, what is what, or have the sense of effective coordination.

—CHESTER I. BARNARD

Definition and Examples

Clarifying is defined as assigning work, providing direction on how to do the work, and communicating a clear understanding of job responsibilities, task objectives, priorities, deadlines, and performance expectations.

The purpose of Clarifying is to guide and coordinate work activities and make sure that people know what to do and how to do it. Clarifying means providing both instruction and relevant information about decisions, plans, and activities.

Examples of Clarifying include:

- Setting specific goals and expected results for a task or project;
- Explaining a person's responsibilities regarding a task or project clearly;
- Specifying an expected date or time for completion of an assignment;
- Responding to misunderstandings or questions about an assignment;
- Explaining what objectives or aspects of the work have the highest priority;
- Telling people what they need to know about your own and others' activities and plans; and
- Following up to ensure progress against plans.

Notes

Clarifying can take a wide variety of forms, but three major categories include:

- Defining roles and responsibilities;
- Setting performance goals and action plans; and
- Assigning work and, when necessary, giving direction on how to do it.

Theories of leadership (Yukl, 1998) suggest that Clarifying will improve employee satisfaction and performance by removing ambiguity relating to roles. Furthermore, performance improves when managers set clear, specific, and realistic goals.

Defining Roles and Responsibilities

It is essential that each direct report or colleague understand what duties, functions, and activities are required to do a job and what results are expected. Even highly competent and motivated people may not achieve high levels of performance if they are confused about their responsibilities and priorities. Confusion about roles results in misdirected effort and neglected responsibilities.

The more complex a job is, the more difficult it is to determine what must be done. You and a direct report are likely to perceive a complex job differently and have different priorities. The direct report may undertake some activities that are inconsistent with your objectives, and, conversely, some activities that you assume are being performed may not be happening at all. Therefore, it is essential for you and your direct reports to agree on job descriptions or roles.

Soon after a person joins your work unit or team or whenever a person's job is altered significantly, have a role-clarification meeting. Begin by reviewing the job description for the position. If no job description exists or if it is outdated, ask the person to prepare one and write one yourself so that you can compare them and identify any gaps or potential areas of disagreement. The job description should include:

- A purpose or mission statement;
- A list of duties and responsibilities;
- Key results for which the person will be held accountable; and
- Priorities for different responsibilities and results.

There is no simple formula for determining priorities, but always consider the importance of an activity for the organization's mission and for the work of your unit and any other work units. Try ranking activities as less important, moderately important, or extremely important priorities.

In the role-clarification meeting, the person's scope of authority and discretion in decision making should be discussed, as well as job duties, responsibilities, and priorities. This is also a good time to check the person's understanding of important organizational rules and policies. Role-clarification meetings also have implications for Coaching, as they can bring out a person's developmental needs as well as the organization's needs.

Listen attentively to the ideas of the person whose role is being clarified, giving his or her concerns and suggestions careful consideration.

For teams that work closely together, hold a group meeting to clarify roles and responsibilities in addition to individual meetings with each team member.

Setting Performance Objectives

During the role-clarification meeting or in a separate goal-setting meeting, jointly set specific performance goals related to key results or outcomes expected. Specific, challenging goals offer several benefits, including:

- Directing efforts toward important duties and responsibilities;
- Encouraging people to find more efficient ways to do the work; and
- Providing a benchmark against which to compare performance.

The number of goals set for each team member in any given performance period (quarterly or annually) should reflect the needs of the organization. In general, five to nine goals are appropriate. The complexity of most jobs will not be covered with fewer than five goals, and more than nine goals is likely to cause confusion about expectations and frustration over competing objectives. Goals should be the following:

- *Aligned:* The goals and strategies of the organization and the team must provide the touchstone.
- *Clear and Specific:* Use simple language, an action verb and a single, specific outcome. Unnecessary details, such as justification for the goal or the action plan needed to attain it, should not be included.
- *Results-Oriented and Verifiable:* A goal should be stated in quantitative terms.
  - Phrases such as "do your best" and "make a substantial improvement" are too vague.
  - The goal can be stated in relative terms, such as "improve production by 10 percent," if necessary, but it is better to use absolute terms such as "sign up twelve new clients by December 1."
  - If an objective measure is not available, use an activity for which successful completion can be verified, such as implementing a policy, training a new employee, attending a workshop, or completing a report.
  - Specify the criteria for determining "successful completion" of an activity in advance.
- *Time-Bound:* A goal statement should include a target date for accomplishment that is specific (June 1), not vague ("by spring" or "as soon as possible"). A specific deadline reduces the chance of misunderstandings.
- *Challenging:* A goal should be difficult enough to be perceived as a challenge. Challenge does not necessarily imply performance improvement. If performance is already at an exceptional level, it may be challenging just to maintain it, especially if conditions are changing.
- *Realistic:* The goal should not be so difficult that it seems impossible or unrealistic. Consider prior performance by the same person, performance by people in comparable positions, available resources, conditions that may affect performance, and the amount of time until the deadline.
- *Relevant:* Goals should be established for primary responsibilities only. When trivial goals are set, they compete for attention, time, and energy that should be applied toward more important goals. State each goal in terms of the desired result, rather than in terms of the action required to attain it.
- *Cost-Effective:* The results should justify the expected costs in resources and work hours. There is usually a trade-off between difficulty and cost; the more difficult a goal is, the more effort and resources needed to achieve it.
- *Mutually Agreed On:* When goals are set mutually, commitment is more likely, and each person knows what the other expects.
- *Written:* The goal statement and supporting action plans should be written, with each person keeping a copy. Having a written "contract" avoids possible misunderstandings.

Assigning Work and Giving Directions

In addition to Clarifying normal duties and responsibilities and setting performance goals, managers or team leaders sometimes must give specific task assignments or provide instruction on how to do a task. These aspects of Clarifying may apply to colleagues or outsiders, such as subcontractors or suppliers, as well as to direct reports or team members.

The following guidelines are helpful for ensuring that directions are understood and accepted:

- *Be polite.* Most people are sensitive about the language and tone in which work assignments are given.

- *Provide appropriate instructions.* If empowerment is an important goal and the person is generally competent, provide only broad guidelines and express confidence that he or she can handle the task well. Ask the person to explain how he or she will do it and later use Coaching to ensure that the job is done well.

- *Explain how to do a task or assignment.* More detailed instructions are needed when the task is complex, the assignment is unusual, or the person is inexperienced. Explain procedures step by step, using clear, simple language and relevant examples. If the task or procedure is very complex, provide written instructions.

- *Give all the information needed.* Include relevant plans or activities and provide the name of a resource or contact person in case of questions or problems.

- *Check for comprehension.* Do not assume that someone automatically understands your directions or instructions. Be alert for signs that the person is confused or has misinterpreted your message. Probe for understanding by asking specific questions about how the person will implement the request.

- *Establish the legitimacy of a request.* An assignment or direction is more likely to be accepted if it is consistent with your authority and with organizational policies and standard procedures. Legitimacy is usually more of an issue with colleagues than with direct reports, but people may question your right to make requests that are unusual or outside of normal channels and procedures. If there is any doubt about your authority to make an assignment or request, explain that you do have the right to make it and why.

- *Explain the reason for a request.* Acceptance is always greater if people understand why they are being asked to do something. Explain why a task or assignment is necessary and important, how it fits with the organization's goals, and why the person is being asked to do it. Understanding the purpose of a request also makes it easier for him or her to deal with unexpected problems that occur.

- *Follow up.* Check to ensure that a request or assignment has been carried out after a reasonable time period. People sometimes delay carrying out an unpleasant or disagreeable request to see if you are really serious about it. It may be put off indefinitely.

When It Is Most Useful

Clarifying is most useful in the following situations:

- When members of the work unit lack the experience and skills;
- When new work unit members need to learn the "rules of road";
- When complex or ambiguous work causes uncertainty about procedures and priorities;
- If a work unit must frequently change its products, services, or timetables to accommodate the needs of clients or customers;
- If the nature of the work or technology is changing;
- When people have interdependent tasks;
- When people are affected by frequent changes in policies, plans, or priorities;
- When the organization is undergoing major changes, such as restructuring, downsizing, or changing strategic direction; or
- When there is a crisis or emergency and people are anxious and concerned about what is happening.

When to Use

Increase or improve your use of Clarifying if:

- Others come to you frequently for information they should already have or for clarification of assignments;
- Tasks or projects are being completed late or inaccurately;
- Team members express confusion about a project's goals or expected results; or
- You are the only source of information others need to solve problems, plan operations, and make decisions.

Tips

Here are some tips for Clarifying:

- Ask people to paraphrase to check their understanding of complicated instructions.
- Ensure that frequently used procedures and policies are available in written form to reinforce learnings and avoid the need to reinvent the wheel.
- Ask people to explain procedures or instructions to others; teaching others is often the best way to learn something.
- Use appropriate body language, such as eye contact, leaning forward, nodding, and smiling, to add clarity and emphasis to a verbal message.
- Be alert for signs of confusion; take the time to repeat yourself if necessary.
- Make yourself available to answer any questions people may have about instructions or assignments.
- Reduce the chances of misinterpretation by confirming important verbal messages, such as a complex new assignment or key policies, in writing.
- Ask someone to summarize the results of a meeting in writing to ensure that you all agree on the outcome.
- Take a business writing course to improve the clarity of your written communications if people seem to misinterpret your instructions.

Readings

Harper, B., & Harper, A. (1992). *Skill-building for self-directed team members.* New York: MW Corporation.

Keffeler, J. (1991). Managing changing organizations. *Vital Speeches of the Day 58,* 92–96.

Kouzes, J., & Posner, B. (1993). *Credibility.* San Francisco: Jossey-Bass.

Locke, E.A., & Latham, G.P. (1990). *A theory of goal setting and task performance.* Englewood Cliffs, NJ: Prentice-Hall.

Luthans, F., Hodgetts, R.M., & Rosenkrantz, S.A. (1988). *Real managers.* Cambridge, MA: Ballinger.

Sayles, L.R. (1993). *The working leader.* New York: The Free Press.

Yukl, G. (1990). *Skills for managers and leaders.* Englewood Cliffs, NJ: Prentice-Hall.

Yukl, G. (1998). *Leadership in organizations.* Englewood Cliffs, NJ: Prentice-Hall.

Planning

People with a knack for strategic planning realize that strategic thinking can no longer be the solitary enterprise of one wise person, that it cannot be done in a closet or on a mountain top, but rather that it is a social, interactive process in which the task is to learn to use the diverse talents and experiences that are available in the organization.

—PETER VAILL

Definition and Examples

Planning is defined as determining long-term objectives and strategies, allocating resources according to priorities, determining how to use personnel and resources efficiently to accomplish a task or project, and determining how to improve coordination, productivity, and effectiveness.

Some examples of Planning include:

- Developing long-range plans for an organizational unit or team that indicate future objectives and strategies;
- Outlining in detail how to accomplish a major task or project by identifying the action steps, then determining when each should be done and by whom;
- Determining what resources are needed to carry out a task or project;
- Setting priorities for different activities and allocating available resources among those activities;
- Eliminating unnecessary activities and procedures to improve efficiency and make better use of resources; and
- Avoiding potential problems that could disrupt operations or jeopardize an important project.

Notes

The results of Planning are obvious: budgets, sales forecasts, production plans, marketing plans, and so on. However, the real key to Planning lies in gaining the commitment of key decision makers and those responsible for implementation. By involving key people in the Planning process, you can develop higher-quality plans and increase the likelihood that they will be implemented successfully. As a result, Planning can lead to higher commitment to overall organizational objectives.

Planning is the bedrock that underlies all work activities. It is critical for the overall efficiency and effectiveness of the work unit—perhaps even to the survival of the organization. It helps a work unit anticipate and adapt to environmental change. If a work unit does no Planning, its future is left to chance.

Planning also helps ensure coordination with other parts of the organization, and helps to integrate the various departmental activities. Planning is closely related to Involving Others and to Clarifying. Two major types of organizational Planning are *strategic* and *operational*.

Strategic Planning

Strategic planning usually refers to long-term activities that bring about the goals of the organization, guide the daily actions of everyone in it, and provide the context for all other organizational activities.

Strategic planning is no longer seen as a linear process that is the exclusive province of senior management. Increasingly, employees at all levels in the organization, especially front-line customer-contact people, contribute to the ongoing process. Strategies can be formulated by a deliberate, formal process or can emerge based on input from people on the front lines. As strategic plans are implemented, their fit with customers, markets, and competitors is continually assessed and adjusted. New strategies evolve as unanticipated market and customer needs are discovered. Current capabilities are matched with market needs and anticipated future trends.

Operational Planning

Operational or action planning is more specific and short-term in nature and is used to outline specific steps to be taken to support the strategic plan. Some examples of operational plans include marketing plans, production plans, and budgets.

Clearly stated goals and objectives are the specific end products of operational planning. These must be tied to the overall direction of the organization and to the specific strategies being pursued.

When It Is Most Useful

Planning is most useful in the following situations:

- When the environment in which the business operates is changing rapidly;
- When a work unit must meet deadlines or budgets and deal effectively with contingencies;
- If work units perform several different types of tasks;
- When work units are composed of members with interdependent tasks that require close coordination;
- When work units rely on one another; or
- When close cooperation is required for the effective service of customers.

When to Use

You may need to increase or improve your use of Planning if you:

- Do not have clearly articulated goals and objectives;
- Frequently do not reach your objectives;
- Find that work appears to be passing between units in a disorganized manner;
- Have frequent operational delays;

- Find that unanticipated problems are impeding the progress of your team or work unit;
- Feel that direct reports or fellow team members are not sure about priorities;
- Experience erosion of market share and profits and loss of competitive position;
- Feel little need for a conscious and deliberate assessment of the situation; or
- Frequently engage in "flying by the seat of your pants."

You may need to use less Planning if you:
- Notice inflexibility in the work unit and are unable to take advantage of unforeseen opportunities;
- Are unable to complete other tasks;.
- Observe that some people self-protectively spend more time Planning than is necessary, although the organization is not obtaining measurable results; or
- Often prepare lengthy reports that end up being filed away or collecting dust.

Tips

Here are some tips for Planning:
- Flexibility is the key to successful planning. Because no one can anticipate all future events, plans should be flexible enough to handle unforeseen events as they occur.
- Strategic planning should include input from all levels in the organization, especially front-line employees, and should be an ongoing process.
- Because change is often disconcerting to people, anticipate resistance and plan ways to overcome it.
- Involve direct reports and colleagues, as well as appropriate people from other work units, in the planning and implementation process. The more people involved, the more perspectives and information that can be brought into play and the deeper the level of commitment to the plan.
- Explain the reasons why certain activities are being implemented and how they relate to the organization's overall strategies and objectives.
- Strive for simplicity. Make plans as simple as possible to ensure greater understanding and commitment.
- Monitor planned activities periodically.

Readings

Gould, M., Campbell, A., & Alexander, M. (1994). *Corporate level strategy: Creating value in the multibusiness company.* New York: John Wiley.

Kaufman, R. (1992). *Strategic planning plus.* Newbury Park, CA: Sage Publications.

Mintzberg, H. (1994). *The rise and fall of strategic planning: Reconceiving roles for planning, plans and planners.* New York: The Free Press.

Perry, L.T., Stott, R.G., & Smallwood, W.N. (1993). *Real-time strategy: Improvising team-based planning for a fast-changing world.* New York: John Wiley.

Rumelt, R.P., Schendel, D.E., & Teece, D.J. (Eds.). (1994). *Fundamental issues in strategy: A research agenda.* Boston: Harvard Business School Press.

Wall, S.J., & Wall, S.R. (1995). The evolution (not the death) of strategy. *Organizational Dynamics, 24*(2), 7–19.

Wall, S.J., & Wall, S.R. (1995). *The new strategists: Creating leaders at all levels.* New York: The Free Press.

Notes

Notes

Notes

Notes

Notes

Notes

Notes

Notes

Notes